Stage 5

Floppy's Phonics

Thelma Page

Group/Guided Reading Notes

Contents

On Safari

Camping

Pirates

To the Rescue!

Monster Party

Exploring Underground

Introduction

Welcome to *Floppy's Phonics* Non-Fiction! This series gives you stunning new photographic non-fiction readers linked to *Letters and Sounds.* Your favourite Oxford Reading Tree characters guide you through a range of exciting topics highlighting key features and asking questions to encourage interaction with the text. Children reinforce and practise their decoding skills whilst encountering a range of non-fiction text types and opportunities to make cross-curricular links.

Phonic development

The Floppy's Phonics Non-Fiction readers support a synthetic phonics approach to early reading skills. The Stage 5 non-fiction readers are specifically designed for children who are working within Phase 5 of *Letters and Sounds.* They develop children's confidence in segmenting and blending phonemes. They revisit all of the sounds covered in the Floppy's Phonics stories at Stage 5 as well as introducing further practice of the phonemes covered in *Letters and Sounds* Phase 5.

The children will benefit most from Floppy's Phonics Non-Fiction Stage 5 if they are beginning to:
- gain familiarity with most of the Phase 5 phonemes, including alternative spellings of long vowel phonemes and other Phase 5 vowel phonemes
- develop an increasing bank of high frequency words.

The Stage 5 non-fiction readers can be read in any order for further practice and consolidation of Phase 5 sounds. You may wish to read the Stage 5 Floppy's Phonics stories with the children to ensure that they are familiar with many of the Phase 5 sounds before they tackle the non-fiction readers.

The non-fiction readers can also be used alongside core *Oxford Reading Tree* and *Songbirds Phonics* titles at Stage 5, or for practice and consolidation after introducing the Phase 5 sounds with other programmes.

Focus phonics

Title	ORT Stage Book Band colour Year group	*Letters* and *Sounds* phase	Phonemes introduced or revisited
On Safari			a (grass) all (tallest) ay (away) ea (leaps) ey (monkey) ind (find) old (cold) ou (you, out) ow (snow, howler) ph (elephant) ue (blue) wh (whale)
Camping			ay (holiday) ou (around, you) i-e (inside) ie (field) ea (seaside) o-e (dome) oul (would) oy (enjoy) wh (which)
Pirates	Stage 5 Green Year 1/P1	5	ay (say) ch (schooner) ea (seas) ew (flew) ey (they, galley) old (gold) ou (found) oy (boy) wh (what)
To the Rescue!			ay (may) ea (breathe) ew (crew) ey (they) ind (kind) ou (trousers) oy (boy) tion (station) u (ambulance) ue (rescue) wh (when)
Monster Party			a-e (paste) ay (way) ea (eat) ew (stew) ey (they) i-e (time) oe (toe) ou (sounds) oul (could) u-e (costume)
Exploring Underground			a-e (cave) ay (today) c (city) e (secrets) ea (reach) ew (new) i-e (mine) o-e (bone) oi (coins) ou (ground, you) ue (blue) wh (what)

Most of the words introduced in Floppy's Phonics Non-Fiction books at Stage 5 are phonically decodable at Letters and Sounds Phase 5. The exceptions are high-frequency tricky words and context words, as listed in the chart on page 4.

High frequency tricky words

The few high frequency words that contain unusual or untaught grapheme-phoneme correspondences are termed 'tricky'. Children also need to become familiar with these as soon as possible, through regular practice.

Context words

Context words are words which may be phonically regular but make use of phonic patterns not yet introduced at the *Letters and Sounds* phase, or are essential for providing meaningful non-fiction information.

High frequency and context words

On Safari	HF tricky words	called
	Context words	Australia
Camping	HF tricky words	could people their
	Context words	
Pirates	HF tricky words	called their
	Context words	pirates
To the Rescue!	HF tricky words	people their
	Context words	lifeguard
Monster Party	HF tricky words	could
	Context words	
Exploring Underground	HF tricky words	could
	Context words	salt

Comprehension strategies

Reading is about making meaning, and it is particularly important that a child's reading books offer opportunities for making sense of text. In spite of a limited vocabulary, all the *Floppy's Phonics* Non-fiction books at Stage 5 are examples of particular genres, e.g. instructions, recount, non-chronological report. They all have features of non-fiction books, such as a contents page, an index and illustrations and photographs with captions and labels that support the text. Some texts also have a simple map feature or quiz.

Book title	Comprehension strategy taught through these Group/Guided Reading Notes				
	Prediction	Questioning	Clarifying	Summarising	Imagining
On Safari	✓	✓	✓	✓	✓
Camping	✓	✓	✓	✓	✓
Pirates	✓	✓	✓	✓	✓
To the Rescue!	✓	✓	✓	✓	
Monster Party	✓	✓	✓	✓	✓
Exploring Underground	✓	✓	✓	✓	✓

Curriculum coverage chart

	Speaking, listening, drama	Reading	Writing
On Safari			
PNS Literacy Framework (Y1)	1.1	(W) 5.1 5.7 (C) 7.1 8.3	9.1
National Curriculum	Level 1		
Scotland: Curriculum for Excellence (P2)	First level: LIT 1-02a	First level: ENG 1-12a, LIT 1-14a, LIT 1-17a	First level: LIT 1-20a, LIT 1-21a, LIT 1-22a, LIT 1-24a, LIT 1-26a
N. Ireland (Y2)	Foundation Stage: Talking and listening	Foundation Stage: Reading	Foundation Stage: Writing
Wales (Key Stage 1)	Range: 1b, c, 2b, 3a, b, c Skills: 1, 2, 3, 4, Language: 2, 3a	Range: 1, 2, 3, 4a, f, g Skills: 1a, b, c, d, 2a, b, c, d, e, 3, 4	Range: 1, 2, 3, 4 Skills: 2, 3, 5, 6, 8a, b, c, d, e
Camping			
PNS Literacy Framework (Y1)	2.2 4.1	(W) 5.2 5.4 (C) 7.2 7.4	11.1
National Curriculum	Level 1		
Scotland: Curriculum for Excellence (P2)	First level: ENG 1-03a, LIT 1-04a, LIT 1-10a	First level: ENG 1-12a, LIT 1-13a, LIT 1-17a	First level: LIT 1-21a, LIT 1-22a, LIT 1-24a
N. Ireland (Y2)	Foundation Stage: Talking and listening	Foundation Stage: Reading	Foundation Stage: Writing
Wales (Key Stage 1)	Range: 1a, 2a, b, 3a, c, 5 Skills: 1, 2, 3 Language: 2	Range: 1, 2, 3, 4a, f, g Skills: 1a, b, c, d 2a, b, c, d, e, 3, 4	Range: 1, 2, 3, 4 Skills: 2, 3, 5, 7a, 8a, b, c, d, e

Curriculum coverage chart

	Speaking, listening, drama	Reading	Writing
Pirates			
PNS Literacy Framework (Y1)	1.2	**W** 5.2 5.3 **C** 7.1 7.2	9.2
National Curriculum	Level 1		
Scotland: Curriculum for Excellence (P2)	First level: ENG 1-03a, LIT 1-06a, LIT 1-10a	First level: ENG 1-12a, LIT 1-13a, ENG 1-17a	First level: LIT 1-22a, LIT 1-23a, LIT 1-24a
N. Ireland (Y2)	Foundation Stage: Talking and listening	Foundation Stage: Reading	Foundation Stage: Writing
Wales (Key Stage 1)	Range: 1a, b, 2a, b, 3a, b, c Skills: 1, 2, 3, 4, 6 Language: 2	Range: 1, 2, 3, 4a, f, g Skills: 1a, b, c, d, 2a, b, c, d, e, 3 4	Range: 1, 2, 3, 4 Skills: 1, 2, 3, 5, 7a, b, 8a, b, c, d, e
To the Rescue!			
PNS Literacy Framework (Y1)	4.1	**W** 5.1 5.4 **C** 7.3 7.4	11.1 11.2
National Curriculum	Level 1		
Scotland: Curriculum for Excellence (P2)	First level: ENG 1-03a, LIT 1-06a	First level: ENG 1-12a, LIT 1-13a, LIT 1-16a, ENG 1-17a	First level: LIT 1-21a, LIT 1-22a, LIT 1-24a, LIT 1-26a
N. Ireland (Y2)	Foundation Stage: Talking and listening	Foundation Stage: Reading	Foundation Stage: Writing
Wales (Key Stage 1)	Range: 1a, b, 2a, b, 3a, c, 5 Skills: 1, 2, 4, 5 Language: 2, 3, 4	Range: 1, 2, 3, 4a, f, g Skills: 1a, b, c, d, 2a, b, c, d, e, 3, 4	Range: 1, 2, 3, 4, 6, 7 Skills: 2, 3, 5, 6, 7a, 8a, b, c, d, e

Curriculum coverage chart

	Speaking, listening, drama	Reading	Writing
Monster Party			
PNS Literacy Framework (Y1)	3.1	(W) 5.1 6.5 (C) 7.2 7.4	9.3 11.1 6.1
National Curriculum	Level 1		
Scotland: Curriculum for Excellence (P2)	First level: LIT 1-02a, LIT 1-09a, LIT 1-10a	First level: ENG 1-12a, LIT 1-13a, ENG 1-17a	First level: Lit 1-23a, LIT 1-26a, LIT 1-28a
N. Ireland (Y1)	Foundation Stage: Talking and listening	Foundation Stage: Reading	Foundation Stage: Writing
Wales (Key Stage 1)	Range: 1, b, c, 2a, 3a, c Skills: 1, 2, 3, 4, 5 Language: 2	Range: 1, 2, 3, 4a, f, g Skills: 1a, b, c, d, 2a, b, c, d, e, 3, 4	Range: 1, 2, 3, 4, 7 Skills: 2, 3, 5, 8a, b, c, d, e
Exploring Underground			
PNS Literacy Framework	3.3	(W) 5.1 6.1 (C) 7.1 7.2	9.1
National Curriculum	Level 1		
Scotland: Curriculum for Excellence (P2)	First level: LIT 1-02a, LIT 1-09a, LIT 1-10a	First level: ENG 1-12a, LIT 1-13a, LIT 1-14a, ENG 1-17a	First level: LIT 1-22a, LIT 1-24a, LIT 1-26a
N. Ireland (Y2)	Foundation Stage: Talking and listening	Foundation Stage: Reading	Foundation Stage: Writing
Wales (Key Stage 1)	Range: 1b, c, 2a, 3a, b, c Skills: 1, 2, 3, 4, 5 Language: 2	Range: 1, 2, 3, 4a, f, g Skills: 1a, b, c, d, 2a, b, c, d, e, 3, 4	Range: 1, 2, 3, 4, 7 Skills: 2, 3, 5, 7a, 8a, b, c, d, e

Key

(C) = Language comprehension Y = Year

(W) = Word recognition

In the designations such as 5.2, the first number represents the strand and the second number the individual objective

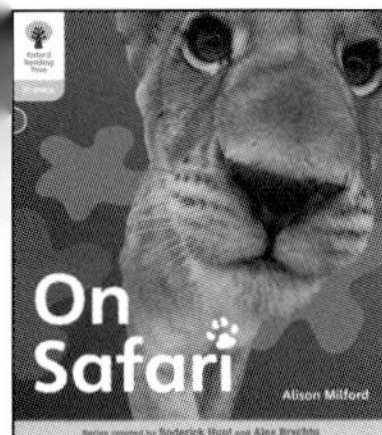

On Safari

C = Language comprehension	**R, AF** = QCA reading assessment focus
W = Word recognition	**W, AF** = QCA writing assessment focus

Focus phonics

Phase 5: a (grass) all (tallest) ay (away) ea (leaps) ey (monkey) ind (find) old (cold) ou (you, out) ow (snow, howler) ph (elephant) ue (blue) wh (whale)

Group or guided reading

Introducing the book

C *(Prediction)* Read the title together, then talk about the meaning of *safari*. Look through the book and ask the children to predict what *safari* means. If necessary explain that a safari is a trip to look for wild animals.

C Look at the contents page. Ask the children to find and read all the names of countries in the list.

C *(Clarifying)* Ask: *Which animals might you find in the countries listed?*

W Read the list of sounds on the contents page. Find a word with *ou* on this page (*sounds*).

Strategy check

Remind the children to break longer words into syllables, then say the letter sounds, e.g. *Arc-tic, an-i-mal.* Help them to practise blending the whole word to say it naturally.

Independent reading

● Ask the children to read the book aloud, praising them for using phonic knowledge to work out new words. If necessary, help with the context word *Australia,* and any other tricky words.

C *(Imagining)* Ask the children to tell you which animals they would most like to see on a safari.

 Check that the children:

- (R, AF1) use phonics as their first approach to decoding new words
- (R, AF3) use the context to help understand the meaning of new words
- (R, AF1) can read common high frequency words on sight.

Returning to the text

C (*Summarising*) Ask children to say what they remember about this book. Which animals interested them most?

C (*Questioning*) Ask: *Do you remember any animals that live in the Arctic?* Look at pages 10 to 13 to check.

C (*Imagining*) Ask the children to imagine what would happen if a polar bear lived in Africa. Encourage them to suggest what the problems might be.

W Find and read a word with *wh* on page 12 (*whale, whistle*). Think of other words that begin with *wh*. Look for a word with *ph* on page 6. Think of other words that use *ph*.

Assessment Check that the children:

- (R, AF3) can use information from the book to make sensible suggestions
- (R, AF1) can find a word with a given phoneme.

Group and independent reading activities

Objective Recognise alternative ways of pronouncing graphemes already taught (5.1).

W **You will need:**. The following graphemes on cards: *s, n, ow, h, l, c, m, sh*.

- Place the cards face up on the table. Ask a child to use the cards to make a word. Read the word together, and write it on a board, e.g. *low*.
- Ask another child to make a different word, e.g. *cow*. Ask: *Does it rhyme with the first word?* If the words rhyme, add the second word beneath the first. If not, begin a new column. Continue until the children have made eight words.
- Read all the words, noticing which words rhyme.
- Add an *r* to *ow*. Discuss the meanings of *row* (argue) and *row* (a boat). Add the word to both columns.

Assessment *(R, AF1)* Could the children differentiate the two ways to pronounce the *ow* phoneme in these words?

Objective Read and spell phonically decodable two-syllable words (5.7).

- **(W) You will need:** A set of these words printed on paper for each child: *Arctic, index, lion, flipper, howler, contents.*

- Ask the children to find the word *Arctic.* Read it together. Clap the syllables: *Arc - tic.* Fold the word to make a crease line between syllables.

- Ask the children to cut the word into syllables, and practise reading and spelling the two halves. Rejoin the word and practise spelling *Arctic.* Then do the same with the other words.

Assessment *(R, AF1)* Could the children divide each word into syllables? Did they learn to spell the words?

Objective Find specific information in simple texts (7.1).

- Use the quiz on pages 22 and 23. Read the questions together, and ask children to answer from memory and their own knowledge.

- Ask them to check their answers in the book.

- Use the index to find the answers to more questions, e.g. *What lives in the Amazon rainforest? What colour is a tomato frog?*

Assessment *(R, AF2)* Were the children able to find answers to the questions by scanning the text?

Objective Distinguish fiction and non-fiction texts and the different purpose for reading them (8.3).

- **You will need:** A pack of *Oxford Reading Tree* stories at Stage 5; a pack of *Floppy Phonics Non-fiction* at Stage 5.

- Mix up the books and spread them out on a table. Ask a child to choose a book and tell you whether it is fiction or non-fiction.

- Discuss the chosen book with the group, asking them how they can tell the difference. Ask questions, e.g. *Both have pictures, how can you tell which one is the story?*

- Make two lists with the headings *Fiction* and *Non-fiction*. Invite the children to suggest features of each type of book, e.g. *photographs, diagrams, contents, index, chapters, titles, etc.* Add the words to the correct list.

- Choose one non-fiction book and find all the features you have mentioned. Do the same for a fiction book.

Assessment *(R, AF2)* Could the children tell the difference between fiction and non-fiction texts? Could they name some of the features of each?

Speaking, listening and drama activities

Objective Describe incidents from their own experience in an audible voice. (1.1)

C *(Clarifying)* Ask the children to help you make a list of animals mentioned in the book. Ask the children to choose an animal from the list to tell you about.

- Ask children to name the animal and say what they found out about it. Ask them to add their own ideas, e.g. *What do you like/dislike about it? What else do you know about this animal? Have you ever seen one? Tell us about it.*

- Ask children to remember to speak in turn and to listen to each other. Encourage them to share incidents from their own experience.

- Praise children for speaking clearly.

Assessment Were the children able to speak confidently and audibly?

Writing activities

Objective Independently choose what to write about, plan and follow it through. (9.1).

C *(Questioning)* Ask the children to choose an animal from the book, and make a labelled drawing, or write and illustrate a few sentences, or make a mini-book about the animal.

- Remind children that they can refer to the book for ideas and spellings.

- Read and display all the work on animals.

- Praise children for explaining and illustrating their ideas clearly.

Assessment *(W AF2, AF3)* Were the children able to choose a format for displaying information and carry it out?

Camping

> **C** = Language comprehension   **R, AF** = QCA reading assessment focus
>
> **W** = Word recognition   **W, AF** = QCA writing assessment focus

Focus phonics

Phase 5: ay (holiday) ou (around, you) i-e (inside) ie (field) ea (seaside) o-e (dome) oul (would) oy (enjoy) wh (which)

Group or guided reading

Introducing the book

C *(Clarifying)* Talk about the front cover picture and read the title together. Ask the children to tell you what they know about going camping. Look through the pictures and let children find a picture of a tent they would like to stay in.

W Find and read *oy* in the sounds box on the contents page. Find a word with /oy/ on page 2 (*enjoy*).

C *(Prediction)* Read the contents page and ask the children to predict which campsite will be the most exciting. Ask them to give their reasons.

Strategy check

Practise segmenting and blending some of the longer words on pages 2 and 3: *animals, sleeping, outside*. Remind children to do this as they read.

Independent reading

- Ask the children to read the book aloud, encouraging them to use phonemes to work out new words.

- Remind them to read longer words in two parts, e.g. *ground-sheet, camp-site*.

C *(Imagining)* Look at the weather today. What would it be like on a campsite? Would you be inside waiting for the rain to stop, or outside having fun?

Assessment Check that the children:

- *(R, AF1)* segment and blend new decodable words.

- *(R, AF1)* can break longer words into syllables to help them read.

- *(R, AF3)* know what the book is about and can make sensible comments.

Returning to the text

C *(Summarising)* Ask the children what they have found out from this book.

C *(Questioning)* Ask: *Which was the most dangerous place to camp?*

W Read the words with *ou* on page 13 (*Scouts, round*). Practise spelling them.

Assessment Check that the children:

- *(R, AF2)* can talk sensibly about the information in this book.

- *(R, AF1)* have begun to recognise words with the same phonic patterns.

Group and independent reading activities

Objective Recognise and use alternative ways of spelling the phonemes already taught and begin to know which words contain which spellings (5.2).

You will need: to prepare a phoneme chart and a list of these words: *day, plate, drain, stay, pain, tray, brain, frame, train, place, play, came, crayon, raining, late, may, aid.*

ai	ay	a-e
drain	day	plate

- Work together to sort the first few words into the right columns. Ask the children to fill in the remaining words independently or in pairs. Read all the words again. Ask volunteers to close their eyes and spell particular words.

Assessment *(R, AF1)* Were the children able to recognise the phonemes and sort them into lists? Could they read and spell the words?

Objective Recognise automatically an increasing number of familiar high frequency words. (5.4)

You will need: These words printed on separate cards: *there* (p4) *different* (p4) *where* (p8) *want* (p8) *could* (p8) *people* (p9) *about* (p16) *when* (p 22).

- Place the cards face down on a table and invite a child to turn over one.

Tell the children the page where the word can be found. Ask a child to find the word in the book and read the whole sentence.

- Continue until all the words have been turned over and found in the book.

- Use the cards as flash cards for a quick recognition game.

Assessment *(R, AF1)* Could the children find and read the words? Did they recognise them out of context on flashcards?

Objective Recognise the main elements that shape different texts (7.4).

- Ask the children how they recognise a non-fiction book. Look through the book to find any features they mention, e.g. *index, contents, headings, photographs*. Use the children's ideas to begin a list.

- Look at the equipment on pages 6 and 7. Ask: *What do we call the writing on these pages?* (Labels). Add *labels* to the list.

- Add more features as you find them in the book, e.g. *captions* on page 19, *instructions* on pages 22–23.

- Choose another Stage 5 book from this series. Look at it together, to find all the features in your list. Add more features (e.g. *textbox*) if you find any.

Assessment *(R, AF4)* Were the children able to suggest some features of non-fiction texts?

Objective Use syntax and context when reading for meaning (7.2)

- On page 16 find the word *hammocks*. Ask the children to find clues in the sentence and in the picture that explain what a hammock is for.

- On page 17, can they explain what a *raft* is?

Assessment *(R, AF1)* Could the children use the context and syntax to understand the meaning of these words?

Speaking, listening and drama activities

Objective Explore familiar themes through improvisation and role play. (4.1)

- Split the children into pairs or small groups and ask each group to choose one of the types of campsite from the book (without telling anyone else).

- Ask the groups to act out what it would be like to camp at their campsite.

- Can the others guess which campsite it was?

Assessment Did the children show in their acting what it was like to go camping?

Writing activities

Objective Compose and write simple sentences independently to communicate meaning (11.1).

- Talk about all the places the book shows people camping: by the sea, at a festival, in a tree, on the side of a mountain, at the North Pole, etc.
- Ask the children to choose the place where they would like to camp. Ask them to write two sentences, saying where they would like to camp, and what would be special about it. They can illustrate their sentences.
- Remind them to use capital letters and full stops.
- Display all the writing in a class *Camping* book.

Assessment *(W, AF6)* Did the sentences make sense? Did the children use punctuation?

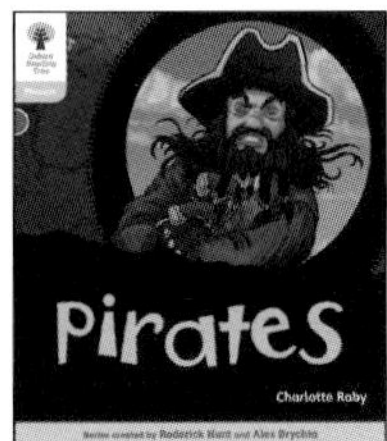

Pirates

> **C** = Language comprehension   **R, AF** = QCA reading assessment focus
>
> **W** = Word recognition   **W, AF** = QCA writing assessment focus

Focus phonics

Phase 5: ay (say) ch (schooner) ea (seas) ew (flew) ey (they, galley) old (gold)
ou (found) oy (boy) wh (what)

Group or guided reading

Introducing the book

C *(Clarifying)* Read the title together. Ask children what they already know about pirates. Find a definition on page 2.

C *(Prediction)* Read the headings listed in the contents. Ask the children to predict what 'Pirate flags' will be about.

W Say the sounds in the sound box. Look for two words with *ea* on page 18.

C *(Imagining)* Ask the children to imagine what a pirate's life would be like. Do they think it would be fun, or dangerous?

W Find *schooner* on page 4. Notice that the *sch* is the same as in *school*.

Strategy check

Remind the children that some longer words are easy to read if you break them into two shorter ones. Find two words in *whatever* (page 3), *inside* (page 5) and *without* (page 6). Remind them to look for more as they read.

Independent reading

- Ask the child to read the book aloud, using phonemes to read independently.
- Help the child to read longer words such as *salmagundi* by saying the sounds one syllable at a time: *sal-ma-gun-di.*

Assessment Check that the children:

- *(R, AF1)* read most of the text independently
- *(R, AF1)* use phonics and syllables to work out words.

Returning to the text

C *(Questioning)* Ask: *Can you name some well-known pirates?* Ask a child to explain how they would use the contents and index to check the names.

C *(Summarising)* Why was the cabin boy left on a desert island? Do you think this was a good thing for him?

C *(Questioning)* Ask: *Why do you think some sailors gave up their ship without fighting?* (Page 6) *What happened to sailors who did not give up?* (Page 14)

W Find and read *called* (page 19) and *their* (page 21). Look, cover, write and check the spellings of these words.

Assessment Check that the children:

- *(R, AF2)* can find answers to questions by referring to the text

- *(R, AF3)* can make inferences and suggest their own ideas

- *(R, AF1)* can read and spell the high frequency words practised.

Group and independent reading activities

Objective Recognise and use alternative ways of spelling the phonemes already taught and begin to know which words contain which spelling alternatives (5.2).

You will need: These words: *stole, clothes, flow, oath, vote, bones, crow, coat, alone, broken, foal, grow, hope, float, low.* A whiteboard and coloured pens.

- Read all the words in the list. Ask the children to tell you the ways that the *oa* sound is written in the words in the list (*o-e, oa, ow*).

- Draw three columns. Choose three colours and write *o-e, oa* and *ow* at the top of the columns, using a different colour for each grapheme.

- Ask children in turn to choose a word from the list, choose the right colour pen, and write the word under the correct grapheme.

- Ask children to think of more words to add to each list.

Assessment *(R, AF1)* Could they distinguish the graphemes and sort the words in columns?

Objective Identify the constituent parts of two-syllable words to support the application of phonic knowledge and skills (5.3).

You will need: These words on strips of paper for each child:

robber, hammock, galley, better, carry, tatty, getting.

- Read all the words together. Begin with *robber.* Clap the syllables: *rob-ber*
- Ask the children to cut the word between the two syllables. Sound-talk the first syllable, then blend it: *r-o-b, rob.* Sound-talk the second syllable, then blend it: *b-er ber.* Rejoin the syllables and say the whole word: *robber.*
- Ask the children to work with a partner to repeat this with all the words.

Assessment *(R, AF1)* Were the children able to separate the words into syllables, and use syllables to read the words?

Objective Find specific information in simple texts (7.1).

You will need: Cards with *Yes* on one side and *No* on the other, one card per pair of children.

- Turn to page 3. Say *Pirates can take a ship. Yes or No?* Children check the text, and show you the right yes/no answer. Continue with the statements below.
- Page 5. *A ship's kitchen is called a galley. Yes or No?*
- Page 6. *The Skull and Crossbones was a pirate ship. Yes or No?*
- Page 10. *There were two female pirates called Jane and Sarah. Yes or No?*
- Page 17. *A pirate was allowed to write. Yes or No?*

Assessment *(R, AF2)* Could the children use the text to find the answer to each question?

Objective Use syntax and context when reading for meaning (7.2).

- Use the context to talk about the meaning of words from the book, e.g. *crew* (page 14), *oath* (page 16), *equal* (page 17), *salmagundi* (page 18). Can the children explain what each word means?

Assessment *(R, AF2)* Could the children use the context to help define the words?

Speaking, listening and drama activities

Objective Retell stories, ordering events using story language (1.2).

- Read the cabin boy's diary again. Begin retelling the story to the group or class in your own words, in the first person as the boy.

- Ask the children to remind you what happened next.
- Tell the whole story together.
- Break the story into sections, e.g. captured by pirates, the pirate's oath, life on board a pirate ship, the diary is found.
- Ask volunteers to tell each part of the story as if they were the boy.

Assessment Did the children contribute ideas and use story-telling language to retell the story?

Writing activities

Objective Use key features of narrative in their own writing (9.2).

- Ask the children to predict what happened next at the end of the cabin boy's story. Did a ship call at the island and take him home? Did he live on the island?
- Ask the children to write a story telling what happened to the boy.
- Encourage the children to use phonics to work out some or all of the letters in the words they write.
- Ask children to read their own story aloud.

Assessment (W, AF1, AF3, AF8) Could the children imagine what happened next? Could they write this part of the story? Did they use phonics to spell some words correctly?

To the Rescue!

> **C** = Language comprehension **R, AF** = QCA reading assessment focus
>
> **W** = Word recognition **W, AF** = QCA writing assessment focus

Focus phonics

Phase 5: ay (may) ea (breathe) ew (crew) ey (they) ind (kind) ou (trousers) oy (boy) tion (station) u (ambulance) ue (rescue) wh (when)

Group or guided reading

Introducing the book

C *(Prediction)* Read the title. Look at the cover and some of the pictures. Ask: *Is this book a story? How can you tell?*

C *(Clarifying)* Ask: *When do people need rescuing? Who comes to rescue us?* Make a list of the children's suggestions.

C *(Summarising)* Read the contents page to see which services are in this book.

W Read the title together, noticing the *ue* in *rescue.*

Strategy check

Remind children to notice punctuation as they read. If they are reading aloud, remind them to use punctuation to help them read with expression.

Independent reading

W Remind children to use syllables to work out new words such as *am-bu-lance.*

C *(Summarising)* Ask the children to explain what one of the rescue services does.

Assessment Check that the children:

- *(R, AF2)* understand what the book is about
- *(R, AF1)* use syllables to work out new words.

Returning to the text

C *(Questioning)* Ask the children to name the rescue services they have read about.

(C) *(Clarifying)* Ask children to explain when people should call 999.

(C) *(Imagining)* Ask the children to imagine that someone is in danger on a beach. *What might be happening? Who would you ask to help?*

(W) Find and read *rescue* and *rescuers* on page 3. Ask the children to tell you how to write *rescues and rescuing*.

Assessment Check that the children:

- *(R, AF2)* have understood what they have read

- *(R, AF1)* can use knowledge of one word to help them write a similar word.

Group and independent reading activities

Objective Recognise and use alternative ways of pronouncing the graphemes already taught (5.1).

You will need: these words on individual cards: *ring, find, quick, child, sink, kind, fill, winch, wild, mind.*

- Begin with *ring.* Show the children the word and sound-talk it together.

- Show them *find* and say the phonemes, initially using the */i/* phoneme as in *ill.* Notice that this does not sound right, so try */i/* as in *ice.* Read the word.

- Sound-talk and read each word in turn.

- Ask children to work in pairs to write the words in two columns, headed *i* as in *ill, i* as in *ice.*

- Ask the children to read and check their lists.

Assessment *(R, AF1)* Were the children able to distinguish the different pronunciations of the grapheme *i*?

Objective Recognise automatically an increasing number of high-frequency words (5.4).

- **You will need:** Separate cards with *they, their* and *there.* Sentences with *their, they,* or *there* missing, e.g. *My bag is over ....; .... went to the shop; They lost .... tickets.*

- Read each sentence in turn. Ask the children to choose the right word to fill the gap. Read the new sentence, then repeat for all three sentences.

- Ask children to work in pairs to write their own sentence with one of the three words missing.
- Let them challenge other pairs to fill the gap with the right word.

Assessment *(R, AF1)* Could the children read the high frequency words on sight? Were they able to select the correct word each time?

Objective Make predictions showing an understanding of ideas (7.3).

- Ask: *Who were the rescue services in this book?* Make a list of the children's suggestions. Check the contents list to see if there were any more.
- For each rescue service, ask the children to suggest more than one situation where that service might be needed.
- Ensure that children understand what each service does to help us.

Assessment *(R, AF2)* Could the children predict situations that indicated that they understood the separate roles and functions of each emergency service?

Objective Recognise the main elements that shape different texts (7.4).

- Ask the children to look through the book and show you features that prove this is a non-fiction text. In this book they can find: *contents, index, titles, fact boxes, labelled pictures, photographs, captions, instructions.*
- Make a list of these features. Ask the children to tell you the page number where each feature can be found. Write the page number beside each item.
- Choose another non-fiction book. Find similar features in this book. Add more features if you find them, e.g. *diagrams, glossary, timeline.*

Assessment *(R, AF2)* Were the children able to recognise features of non-fiction texts?

Speaking, listening and drama activities

Objective Explore familiar themes through improvisation and role-play. (4.1)

- Talk about a situation in the book, e.g. the car stuck in the snow on page 5. Ask the children to imagine what might have happened. Ask: *How did the people get stuck? What did they do to get help? What did the fire-fighters do when they arrived?*

- Act out the scenario. Decide who will be in the car, who will use the phone and who will be the fire-fighters. Encourage the children to improvise dialogue.
- Repeat the scenario with different children, or develop a new one, e.g. around the boy on page 10.
- Praise children for imagining the emergency and for creating a short scene.

Assessment Were the children able to improvise a situation and take roles?

Writing activities

Objective Compose and write simple sentences independently to create meaning (11.1). Use capital letters and full stops when punctuating simple sentences (11.2)

- Plan and make a display entitled *Rescue!*
- Ask children to work in pairs to plan a poster to show the work of one of the rescue services.
- Ask them to give the poster a title and write one or two sentences to say what the service does. Remind them to use capital letters and full stops correctly.
- Ask them to illustrate the poster to make it look interesting.
- Ask children to read their own poster to the class. Display all the posters.

Assessment *(W, AF2)* Were the children able to write simple sentences about the rescue service chosen? Did they use punctuation correctly?

Monster Party

> **C** = Language comprehension *R, AF* = QCA reading assessment focus
>
> **W** = Word recognition *W, AF* = QCA writing assessment focus

Focus phonics

Phase 5: a-e (paste) ay (way) ea (eat) ew (stew) ey (they) i-e (time) oe (toe) ou (sounds) oul (could) u-e (costume)

Group or guided reading

Introducing the book

C *(Prediction)* Read the title and look at the cover picture. Read the blurb on the back cover. Ask children to predict what the book will be about.

W Use fingers to count the phonemes in monster and party as you say them: m-o-n-s-t-er p-ar-t-y

C *(Clarifying)* Ask children to talk about their own parties. Ask: *Has anyone ever had a monster party, or a Hallowe'en party? How did people dress?*

C *(Imagining)* Ask: *If you were going to monster party, how would you dress up?*

Strategy check

Remind the children to use the sense of the sentence as well as sounds to make sure that the text makes sense.

Independent reading

C *(Questioning)* Looking at page 12, ask: *Can you explain what* costume *means? Can you find another word for* costume *on this page?*

W Notice whether children recognise high frequency words such as *like, them, make, some* on sight.

Assessment Check that the children:

- *(R, AF1)* read high frequency words on sight
- *(R, AF2)* can explain the meaning of selected words.

Returning to the text

C *(Imagining) Can you tell me what you need to think about if you are planning a party?* Turn back to page 3 and read the list. *Is there anything else you need to do?* (e.g. write invitations)

C *(Questioning)* Ask: *How can we find out about party games in this book?* (Use the contents or index.) Ask: *How many games can you find?*

C *(Summarising)* Ask: *Which did you think were the best ideas?* Find the page and ask the child to explain the ideas they liked.

W Look for words with *ou* on page 6 (*sprouts, sound, you.*) Notice two different ways to pronounce *ou*.

Assessment Check that the children:

- *(R, AF2)* understood how to find information in this book
- *(R, AF6)* could express a personal response to the ideas
- *(R, AF1)* can recognise the variations in pronouncing *ou* in these words.

Group and independent reading activities

Objective Recognise and use alternative ways of spelling the phonemes already taught and begin to know which words contain which spelling alternatives (5.2).

You will need: Cards with the graphemes *ie, ue, oe* on and cards with the consonants *b, c, f, k, n, t* for each pair of children:

- Read *ie, ue,* and *oe* together. Write this list of words on a board: *fine, bike; bone, note; tube, cute.*
- Give each pair a set of graphemes and a set of consonants.
- Choose a word, e.g. *fine,* and ask the children to say the phonemes in order, *f- ie- n.* Using the cards make the word using the consonants and grapheme *ie.*
- Look at the spelling of *fine* in the list on the board and notice that the *ie* sound has been split. Cut the *ie* grapheme card into *i* and *e.* Make the word *fine* with the correct spelling. Ask the children to make *bike.*

- Use the consonants and vowel grapheme cards to make more words.

Assessment *(R, AF1)* Did the children use the cards to spell the words correctly?

Objective Use knowledge of common inflections in spelling, such as plurals (6.5).

- Find *balloons* on page 3. Say, *if there was only one, what would the word be? How do we change the spelling?* Write *balloon* and *balloons*.
- Look in the book for more words ending in *s*. Decide if the word means more than one of something. If so, say what the word would be for just one.
- Ask children to spell or write: *tin, tins; cat, cats; car, cars; bun, buns; dog, dogs; pet, pets.* Praise the children spelling accurately.

Assessment *(R, AF1)* Did the children spell the words correctly?

Objective Recognise the main elements that shape different texts (7.4)

- Ask the children to find a set of instructions in the book. Ask: *How do you know these are instructions?*
- Make a list of the children's suggestions, e.g. *they tell you what to do, they tell you things in the right order.*
- Turn to page 13. Notice the words '*How to ...*' in the title. Read all the instructions and ask: *Do you think these instructions are easy to understand? Do they tell you clearly what to do? How do the pictures help?*
- Look at pages 14 and 15. Read the first word in each numbered instruction. Each one is a command. Make a list of the command words.

Assessment *(R, AF4)* Could the children identify and comment on the organization of instruction texts?

Objective Use syntax and context when reading for meaning (7.2)

- In pairs, ask the children to think of words to use instead of *big* (page 12), *stuff (page 12), cute* (page 16) and *best* (page 23).

Assessment *(R, AF1, AF3)* Could the children use the context to suggest alternative words?

Speaking, listening and drama activities

Objective Take turns to speak, listen to others' suggestions and talk about what they are going to do. (3.1)

- Ask the children to talk about parties they have been to. *What was the best thing? What was the worst thing?*
- As a group agree on all the good things about parties, e.g. the guests, the food, the games, etc.
- Children should work with a partner to decide three rules for a great party. Each pair reports back to the class with their rules.

Assessment Did the children listen to each other's ideas? Did they make decisions and report back to the class?

Writing activities

Objective Convey information and ideas in a simple non-narrative form (9.3). Use capital letters and full stops when punctuating simple sentences (11.2). Spell new words using phonics as the prime approach (6.1)

You will need: A zigzag book for each child with four pages.

- Remind children of the rules they came up with in the speaking and listening activity.
- Working in pairs, ask them to think of a title for their party, e.g. monster party, super-hero party, princess party, etc.
- Ask them to choose three rules for having a great party and to write and illustrate the rules in their zigzag books.
- Remind them to use capital letters and full stops correctly.
- Praise them for attempting spellings independently or conferring with their partner.

Assessment *(W, AF2, AF6, AF8)* Could the children convey the rules for their party clearly? Did they punctuate sentences correctly? Did they use some correct spelling?

Exploring Underground

> **C** = Language comprehension   **R, AF** = QCA reading assessment focus
>
> **W** = Word recognition   **W, AF** = QCA writing assessment focus

Focus phonics

Phase 5: a-e (cave) ay (today) c (city) e (secrets) ea (reach) ew (new) i-e (mine) o-e (bone) oi (coins) ou (ground, you) ue (blue) wh (what)

Group or guided reading

Introducing the book

C *(Prediction)* Read the title. Ask: *Do you know what is under the ground?* Ask the children to predict what they might find in this book. Compare the contents list with your predictions.

C *(Clarifying)* Read pages 2 and 3. Ask the children to suggest some more ideas for things that could be under the ground.

W Look at pages 4 and 5. Find the words *stalagmite* and *stalactite.* Use syllables to work out how to read these words: *sta-lag-mite, sta-lac-tite.*

Strategy check

Remind the children to use words they already know to help them work out new words, e.g. *swim* in *swimming*; *under* in *underneath.*

Independent reading

● Remind them to use the labels in photographs to understand words such as *stalagmite.*

C *(Summarising)* Ask the child to tell you about three places where they might be able to go under the ground.

Assessment Check that the children:

● *(R, AF1)* use phonics to segment, then blend new words

● *(R, AF2)* can use photographs and labels to help them understand new words

● *(R AF2)* can tell you about places described in the book.

Returning to the text

C *(Summarising)* Turn back to pages 2 and 3. Ask: *Did you find all these suggestions in the book? Which one was not in the book?*

C *(Imagining)* Ask*: Can you think of anything else that could have been in this book?* (e.g. animals that live underground, fossils)

C *(Questioning)* Ask: *Can people who are not miners visit a mine?* Find the page that shows us.

W Ask the children to show you a word they found difficult to read. Turn to the page and explore different ways of reading the word, e.g. phonics, syllables, part of the word you already know.

Assessment Check that the children:

- *(R, AF2)* can answer questions about the book
- *(R, AF1)* can use a variety of strategies to work out new words.

Group and independent reading activities

Objective Recognise and use alternative ways of pronouncing the graphemes already taught (5.1).

You will need: these words on individual cards: *city, cities, castle, cave, coal, cavern, circle, circus, centre, celery, cereal, cycle, cyclist, case, coffee, cool, count, car.*

- Read the words in turn. After reading, ask the children to sort the words into two sets. Ask them to tell you the rule they have used for sorting the words.
- If they have chosen any other rule than the two sounds of *c*, ask them to use this rule to sort the words again.

Assessment *(R, AF1)* Could the children distinguish between the two phonemes for *c*?

Objective Spell new words using phonics as the prime approach (6.1).

- Help the children to practise spelling some new or tricky words from the book, e.g. *under, ground, coins, fantastic, different, miner, statue, electricity, railways, window.*

- Show the children how to use sound buttons to match the words, marking the phonemes, e.g.

under *ground* *coin* *fantastic*

- In pairs, ask the children to choose four words from the book and write them with sound buttons, saying the phonemes as they do so.
- Ask each pair to practise spelling their four words. Then ask them to spell one word each to the group. Praise the children for excellent spelling.

Assessment *(R, AF1)* Were the children able to use sound buttons to help them spell words from the book?

Objective Find specific information in simple texts (7.1).

- Read the book together.
- Ask each child to think of a question that can be answered in this book, e.g. *Where can you find a stalactite? Which page shows a house underground?*
- Ask the group to answer each child's question in turn by finding the page in the book.
- If children find it hard to invent questions, think of some yourself and ask the children to find the answers.

Assessment *(R, AF2)* Could the children use the book to answer the questions?

Objective Use syntax and context when reading for meaning (7.2).

- Ask children to work in pairs. Ask each pair to explain one of these topics to the group: *mines, caves, houses under the ground.*
- Ask them to use the contents and index to find and read the right pages.
- Remind them that there is information in the pictures, as well as the words.
- Ask them to explain to the rest of the class what they have found out.

Assessment *(R, AF2)* Could the children use the information in the book to describe their chosen topic clearly?

Speaking, listening and drama activities

Objective Explain their views to others in a small group, decide how to report the group's views to the class (3.3).

- In groups of two, three or four, ask children to tell each other when they have been underground, e.g. tube trains, channel tunnel, other tunnels, caves or mines.
- If children have not been underground, ask them to tell the others if they think they would like it or not.
- Ask them to report back to the class saying whether their group thought being underground was fun and exciting, or whether they thought it was dark and scary.

Assessment Were the children able to talk to the group about their own experiences? Could they report the group's feelings to the class?

Writing activities

Objective Independently choose what to write about, plan and follow it through (9.1)

- Ask the children to choose between *Caves, Mines* and *Houses Underground* as titles for a piece of writing.
- Ask them to decide how to write about the chosen topic, e.g. in a few sentences with a picture, as a labelled drawing or as a series of pictures with labels or captions.
- Encourage them to find and use information from the book but write in their own words.

Assessment *(W, AF 7)* Were the children able to make independent choices and write using their own words?